Introduction

Kellie Castle and Garden is a place that can truly claim to be the setting for a 'Sleeping Beauty' fable. Here in this tranquil environment, hidden away in a relatively undiscovered but exceptionally lovely corner of Scotland, time seems to have stood still. Kellie is unique in that it escaped the alterations many owners made to their great houses in the nineteenth century: it therefore retains much of its seventeenth-century structure and many of its exquisite interiors, which are of major importance in the history of the decorative arts in Scotland.

The preservation of so many traditional elements made Kellie a vital source of inspiration for the Lorimers, an artistic Edinburgh family who fell in love with it and spent all their summers here in the late nineteenth century. In particular, the castle and its surroundings imbued the young Robert Lorimer with a passion for vernacular Scottish architecture that he took into the Arts & Crafts movement, in which he was a seminal figure.

The early days

The first mention of Kellie occurs about 1150: in a charter of the Scottish King David I of that date, Malmure, thane of Kellie, is recorded as a witness. The next recorded owner was Robert of Lundin, the illegitimate son of King William the Lion (reigned 1165-1214). By the early thirteenth century, Kellie had passed into the ownership of the Siward family, whose ancestors had come from Northumbria around 1057 to help Malcolm Canmore win the Scottish throne from Macbeth. Sir William Siward held a charter for the barony of Kellie from the Scottish King Robert I (Robert the Bruce).

William was succeeded by Richard Siward, who was captured by Edward I's army in 1296 at the battle of Dunbar, the beginning of the Wars of Independence, when many Scottish nobles were fighting to overthrow English domination. He subsequently became a prominent member of Edward's administration in Scotland. After Robert the Bruce's victory over the English at Bannockburn in 1314, Richard Siward's estates were confiscated: however, Kellie did pass into the hands of his daughter Elena – perhaps because she was linked through marriage to the Scottish king. By 1360 Elena's husband Isaac Maxwell had died, and in this year she assigned the Kellie estates to her cousin, Walter Oliphant, who was married to a daughter of Robert the Bruce and brother-in-law to King David II. Thus began 250 years of Oliphant ownership of the castle.

The Oliphants

Walter was one of the most prominent landowners in Scotland. In 1378 he resigned Kellie, one of his minor holdings, to his second son, and the estate was owned by a cadet branch of the Oliphants for almost two centuries. We know little about them, until the succession in 1537 of Sir Alexander Oliphant, whose interesting appearances in records reveal that he prosecuted a bitter feud with the Prioress of North Berwick, and that he had his marriage to the daughter of the Earl of Rothes annulled in 1550 when he discovered she was illegitimate.

He played safe the following year by marrying his cousin Katherine Oliphant. She was daughter of the head of the Oliphant clan and this marriage again brought Kellie back to the main branch of the family: in 1552 Alexander conveyed the estate to Laurence, third Lord Oliphant. Closer family heirs disputed this after his death, but in vain – though fortunate for Kellie, since the richer Oliphants were better placed to develop the castle. It is likely that Kellie was not their principal residence, but that its main purpose was as a fortified stronghold. They remained owners until the seventeenth century, and made most of the changes that created the castle you see today.

Opposite page: A Country Life photograph of Kellie Castle in 1906, entitled 'the earliest tower'

Opposite bottom: In this document, now in the Oliphant Papers at the National Library of Scotland, the name of Walter Oliphant appears for the first time. It is the 'resignation' by Elena Maxwell of the lands of Kellie to the king, for onward assignation to Walter, Elena's cousin: it is dated 30 January 1360

Below: Katherine Oliphant, who married her cousin Alexander in 1551. This portrait by an unknown artist is dated 1595, after Alexander's death and her remarriage to George Dundas

Bottom of page: Charter, dated 20 October 1378, of King Robert II 'to Walter Olyfaunt of the lands and barony of Kellie and Petkery'. This Walter was the second Oliphant to own Kellie

Laurence, fourth Lord Oliphant, who succeeded to Kellie in 1566, was a prominent supporter of Mary, Queen of Scots and the Earl of Bothwell, whom he had helped to acquit of the murder of Darnley. In May 1567, Laurence was present at Mary's marriage to Bothwell at the Palace of Holyroodhouse. The following year, he was one of the 20 lords who wrote to Queen Elizabeth of England pleading for Mary's release from prison.

Evidence indicates that he extended the east tower with two upper floors in 1573. This date, together with his wife Lady Margaret Hay's initials, are carved high up on the south face of the tower, suggesting that Kellie may have been her 'jointure' house – a dwelling given to a wife on marriage for her to use should her husband die.

Laurence, fifth Lord Oliphant, succeeded his grandfather in 1593. By 1606, he had completed a third tower at the south-west, refashioned the older tower to the north and remodelled the central portion which unites the north-west and east towers and marks the architectural transition from tower house to mansion house. The dormer heads on the south and west façades of the castle bear the Oliphant arms and the date 1606. It is likely that Laurence could afford this work because he had received vast funds from his father-in-law in return for allowing his wife part of the revenue from the Kellie estate.

The fifth lord seems to have had a volatile temperament: a letter of May 1617 from Lord Binning to King James reported how Laurence had stabbed his kinsman, Patrick Oliphant, without provocation, at Dupplin Castle:

'Standing in the hall before the fyre efter they had sowped, Patriks doublet and cloathes being lowse, the Lord Oliphant upon the suddane without any schew of displeasour in wourdis or countenance, gave to Patrik ane great and dangerous wound in the bellie … which is judged to be most deadlie.'

His excesses also extended to squandering his inheritance and a huge dowry from his wife. In 1613, his mounting debts forced him to sell Kellie to Sir Thomas Erskine, Viscount Fentoun.

Above: This document of 22 January 1603 is a demand by Laurence, fifth Lord Oliphant, for rent from his tenants at Kellie

Below: Charter under the Great Seal to Thomas, Viscount Fentoun … of the lands and barony of Kellie, dated 13 July 1613

The Earls of Kellie

Sir Thomas had received various honours from King James VI for having helped to avert the attempt on the monarch's life in Perth in 1600 by conspirators led by the Earl of Gowrie. One of these rewards was the Earldom of Kellie, which the king bestowed on him in 1619. It is believed that James stayed the night at Kellie in 1617, during his only return visit to Scotland since becoming King of England. Sir Thomas' main contribution to the castle was the beautiful plaster ceiling in the library, which bears the date '1617' and his initials 'T V F'. Thomas died in 1639 and his gravestone can still be seen set in the north wall of Pittenweem church, only three miles from Kellie.

Alexander, the third Earl, Thomas' grandson, was a staunch supporter of Charles II during the Civil War and fought with him at the battle of Worcester in 1651. After a brief imprisonment in the Tower he was sent into exile in Holland, where he married Lady Mary Kilpatrick, daughter of a Dutch colonel. After seven years' banishment, he was given leave by the English to return briefly to put his estates in order, and brought his wife to Kellie for the first time, landing at nearby Pittenweem. According to a contemporary source, 'the said house [was] repaired by his sisters a little before their coming'. On the Restoration of Charles II in 1660 Alexander's estates were fully restored to him, and he returned to live permanently at Kellie.

Alexander was responsible for the superb plaster ceilings in the castle. His and his first wife's coats-of-arms are on the Dining Room ceiling; those of Alexander and his second wife Mary Dalzell can be seen in the impressive plaster ceilings of the Great Hall (now the Drawing Room) and in the Earl's Room immediately above it.

Alexander, the fifth Earl, continued the family tradition of support for the House of Stuart. He led a small band from Fife to join Prince Charles Edward ('Bonnie Prince Charlie'), was made a colonel in the Jacobite army and saw action in the ill-fated campaign that ended at Culloden in 1746. Eventually captured after several months evading English troops, Alexander was sentenced to three years' imprisonment in Edinburgh Castle for his part in the Rising.

Above: On the run from government soldiers after the battle of Culloden, Alexander, fifth Earl of Kellie, hid for a whole summer in an old beech tree in the grounds of Kellie Castle. The tree was destroyed by lightning in 1887, but John Henry Lorimer's painting of it hangs in the castle

Above: Part of a letter from Alexander, fourth Earl of Kellie, to the Earl of Mar, dated 8 June 1707

Below: Act of King George II in February 1753, depriving of their civil rights those lords convicted of treason for having supported the Jacobite Rising in 1745-6. Alexander, Earl of Kellie, comes first in the list

George the Second by the Grace of God

Enlightenment luminaries

'Loudness … enthusiasm, announce the Earl of Kellie'

Thomas Erskine, sixth Earl of Kellie, was Grand Master of the English and Scottish Masonic Lodges simultaneously. His Edinburgh home was a meeting place for men of letters during the Scottish Enlightenment of the eighteenth century.

Thomas was one of the most significant British composers of the eighteenth century. He studied composition in Mannheim under the innovative Johann Stamitz, and his symphonies were an important influence on contemporary musical taste. Thomas Robertson, writing in 1784, said of his work: 'Elegance is mingled with fire … While others please and amuse, it is his province to rouse … Loudness, rapidity, enthusiasm, announce the Earl of Kellie.' Also a renowned performer, he was known as 'Fiddler Tam' because of his skill on the violin.

I have lost my Stomach

Pub: June 1st 1780.

The famous diarist James Boswell had a warm regard for the sixth Earl, whom he described approvingly as 'a gamester, a nobleman and a musical composer'. Thomas was certainly involved in many colourful aspects of social life in Enlightenment Edinburgh. He founded the Capillaire Club, devoted to the drinking of a liqueur of that name, and it is said that his complexion became so ruddy through his love of strong drink that a friend invited him to 'look over the wall upon my cucumber bed, which has had no sun this year'. He also belonged to the Beggar's Benison Club, an all-male society devoted to sexual pleasure, which was founded about 1732 in Anstruther, Fife, but spread rapidly to Edinburgh, Glasgow, London and as far as St Petersburg. Members – who included leading merchants, aristocrats and even, later, King George IV – claimed an ancient origin for their club, based on the unlikely hypothesis that the Garden of Eden had been situated in Anstruther. The club's name derived from a blessing traditionally bestowed on James V by a young beggar woman: 'May your purse ne'er be toom [empty] /And your horn aye in bloom'.

Another important figure in the Edinburgh establishment of this time, the famous publisher Archibald Constable, also came from Kellie. He was the son of the Earl's factor, and was born in Crow Wood House in the castle grounds, now a gardener's cottage. Constable published most of Sir Walter Scott's works, as well as the influential journals *The Scots Magazine* and *Edinburgh Review*. In 1814 he acquired the *Encyclopedia Britannica*, which still contains an entry about him. His firm, however, went bankrupt in 1826, and its founder died the following year. It was re-established by Archibald's grandson in 1890, and continues to flourish.

Thomas, sixth Earl of Kellie (top) by Robert Home (1752-1834), and in a caricature, probably by James Gillray (1757-1815), entitled 'I have lost my stomach'. Bottom: Portrait of Archibald Constable by Andrew Geddes, 1813

'Ruin grimly dwelt in its deserted halls'

Thomas was succeeded in 1781 by his brother Archibald, the seventh Earl and the last to live at Kellie. It was almost certainly he who commissioned the Drawing-Room and Dining-Room mantelshelves. Professor Lorimer blamed him for the supposed removal of much of the original woodwork in the castle, which he termed an 'act of barbarism'. He wrote: 'It is probable that we owe more to the poverty of this excellent nobleman than to his taste ... it can scarcely be doubted that, if he could have afforded it, he would have pulled down Kellie Castle and built in its stead a large square tea-box.'

With Archibald's death in 1797 the direct line came to an end and the earldom passed to a distant cousin: the castle and grounds fell into neglect. A succession of childless inheritors followed until, in 1829, there were no immediate heirs. A 'muckle roup' or auction of the castle's contents was held and the great home was virtually abandoned. The title was claimed by John Miller Francis Erskine, ninth Earl of Mar, as collateral male heir (a descendant from the same ancestor through a different line). He had to go back more than 200 years to prove a common ancestor but in September 1835 judgement was found in his favour, by which he became eleventh Earl of Kellie.

For a few years in the 1840s the manager of a coal pit, opened up on an adjoining field, lived here with his family. By the 1860s the Great Hall and Withdrawing Room were in use as a barn. The next 50 years at Kellie was a time when, as vividly described in a 1906 edition of the *East of Fife Record*: 'ruin grimly dwelt in its deserted halls'.

Above: John Miller Francis Erskine, who won a lawsuit to become eleventh Earl of Kellie, as painted by his butler about 1840; and a section of the House of Lords judgement on his claim

The last of the line

The tenth Earl of Kellie was the last to claim direct succession to the title. He was lord-lieutenant of the county of Fife and so well respected in the area that, in 1824, a committee of local 'noblemen and gentlemen' commissioned his portrait from David Wilkie (1785-1841), the most celebrated Scottish painter of his time. Wilkie, who was born in Fife, was paid from subscriptions solicited by the committee. The Earl died in 1829, so soon after the portrait was finished that Lady Kellie could not bear to see it, her son writing: 'She retains too lively a recollection of him & his many amiable qualities [and is] ... fearfull that the sight of his Portrait might be too much for her frail frame to bear.' The vigorous painting still hangs in the County Hall in Cupar, Fife.

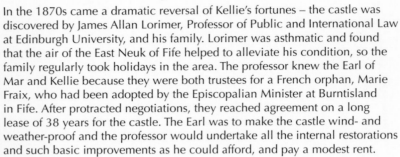

'Preserved with loving care'

In the 1870s came a dramatic reversal of Kellie's fortunes – the castle was discovered by James Allan Lorimer, Professor of Public and International Law at Edinburgh University, and his family. Lorimer was asthmatic and found that the air of the East Neuk of Fife helped to alleviate his condition, so the family regularly took holidays in the area. The professor knew the Earl of Mar and Kellie because they were both trustees for a French orphan, Marie Fraix, who had been adopted by the Episcopalian Minister at Burntisland in Fife. After protracted negotiations, they reached agreement on a long lease of 38 years for the castle. The Earl was to make the castle wind- and weather-proof and the professor would undertake all the internal restorations and such basic improvements as he could afford, and pay a modest rent.

In September 1878 the Lorimer family slept there for the first time: the professor, his young wife Hannah and their six children – James, John Henry, Hannah, Alice, Louise and Robert. Louise later recorded that neighbouring landowners 'thought us daft' for taking on a property in such a state of near-ruin. She wrote of Kellie:

'It was left to the rooks and the owls who built in its crumbling chimneys and dropped down piles of twigs which reached out into the rooms. Great holes let the rain and snow through the roofs, many of the floors had become unsafe, every pane of glass was broken, and swallows built in the coronets on the ceilings, while the ceilings themselves sagged and in some cases fell into the rooms ... '

Louise's vivid description is echoed in the Latin inscription over the entrance door that commemorates the Lorimers' rescue: *'Hoc domicilium corvis et bubonibus ereptum honesto inter labores otio consecratum est'* ('This mansion snatched from rooks and owls is dedicated to honest ease amidst labours'). The repairs organised by Professor Lorimer were necessarily limited, since Kellie was not a year-round home for the family – and perhaps he feared the Earls would reclaim the castle if it was made too desirable! Living conditions were spartan: initially only the Dining Room and some of the east wing were habitable. An earth closet in the garden served as a toilet for the men, there was no running water for the baths and no electric light, only candles and paraffin lamps.

Top: Professor Lorimer at the door of Kellie Castle

Middle: The French orphan Marie Fraix, the link between Professor Lorimer and the Earl of Mar and Kellie, later married the Comte de l'Espinasse. This is her portrait by John Henry Lorimer, which hangs at Kellie

Bottom: An early drawing by John Henry Lorimer of his brother Robert reading to their father, the professor, at Kellie

Outside, the major repairs were to the roofs, chimney stacks and windows; inside, extensive and skilful repairs were needed to panelling, flooring and plasterwork.

Professor Lorimer engaged John Currie, a local architect from Elie, to supervise the work. The stone stairs were carefully repaired, and one of the rooms in the north-west tower was fitted up as a studio for John Henry Lorimer, by enlarging the existing window and putting in skylights. The once-magnificent plasterwork in the Vine Room was carefully restored by the Williamsons of Pittenweem and Cellardyke, who took casts from the unaffected parts to reconstruct the sections destroyed by damp. They also restored half the wreath round the central coat-of-arms in the Great Hall, all their work showing great sensitivity to the original craftsmanship.

Professor Lorimer carried out painstaking research into the history of Kellie in order to inform his repairs. His handwritten investigations are bound in a red leather-covered volume known as *The Red Book of Kellie*. David MacGibbon and Thomas Ross used some of Lorimer's research in their entry on Kellie in their definitive book on the history of vernacular architecture, *Castellated and Domestic Architecture of Scotland*, published in 1887. The *East of Fife Record* commented of the restoration work: 'With Professor Lorimer there was no wholesale gutting out, every bit of antiquity was preserved with loving care.'

Top: Local children – including possibly some of the young Lorimers – outside the castle in 1896

Above: The south front of the castle photographed for Country Life *in 1906, showing doves in the doocot and a bench designed by the young Robert Lorimer*

Under the influence of Kellie: Robert & John Henry Lorimer

Their family's holiday home undoubtedly had a profound effect on the Lorimer children during their formative years. Kellie inspired the young Robert's early interest in architecture; at the age of fourteen, he helped with his father's restoration of the castle, and learned the skills of plastering, carpentry and stonemasonry. He went on to become a seminal figure in the development of Scottish vernacular architecture. The illustration on the opposite page shows his drawing of an elevation at Kellie while he was serving his apprenticeship: he also drew plans for the garden.

Setting up his own practice in Edinburgh in 1893, Robert Lorimer was strongly influenced by the ideas of William Morris and the Arts & Crafts school, which sought to revive traditional building crafts and the use of local materials. He gathered around him a highly talented group of artists and craftsmen.

Lorimer adopted many elements of the late sixteenth- and early seventeenth-century architecture of Kellie in his designs for large country houses such as Rowallan (1902) and Formakin (1908). He restored two Fife properties near Kellie: Earlshall in 1899, and Hill of Tarvit (which was practically rebuilt) in 1905. Six years later, he was knighted for his design for the Thistle Chapel, St Giles' Cathedral, Edinburgh. He is perhaps most famous for his Scottish National War Memorial in Edinburgh Castle: he followed this with countless other smaller memorials both in Britain and abroad, for the Imperial War Graves Commission.

John Henry, Robert's elder brother, trained at the Royal Scottish Academy in Edinburgh under the famous painter Sir William McTaggart and then in Paris. He became a distinguished painter of portraits and contemporary genre (everyday scenes). His best-known work is *The Ordination of the Elders*, which hangs in the National Gallery of Scotland. Although he travelled widely in Europe and North Africa, many of his paintings are based on Kellie, and several of them are on display in the castle today.

Opposite page: Brothers Robert (left) and John Henry Lorimer

Top: Robert drew this elevation of the castle as an architectural apprentice in 1887

Right: John Henry's painting, Sunlight in a Scottish Room, *which depicts the Drawing Room at Kellie and hangs in the John Henry Lorimer Room*

Rescued once more

Professor Lorimer died in 1890 but the family continued to spend the summer at Kellie for many years: his widow last stayed there in 1916. Their son John Henry took up the tenancy after his mother's death and lived there from early spring till late autumn each year, until he died at the age of eighty in 1936. On his death, a second 'muckle roup' took place. The entire contents of the house were sold and it seemed that Kellie was once again doomed to neglect. Then, in another dramatic reversal of fortune, John Henry's nephew Hew and his wife Mary McLeod Wylie took over the lease in 1937.

Hew's father Robert Lorimer had been asked by the Earl of Mar and Kellie in 1916 to design an extensive restoration of Kellie Castle, but the First World War had prevented this going ahead. Hew, however, had inherited his father's creative talents and had become a monumental stone carver. Mary, who had met Hew at the Edinburgh School of Art, had pursued her art studies at the Slade in London, and in Paris, Italy, Germany and Poland.

When Hew and Mary moved to Kellie, the castle was empty and neglected. With her sound instinct for colour, texture and character, Mary set about bringing it back to life, furnishing it with pieces inherited by Hew from his father's collections, together with other carefully chosen purchases. She painted, embroidered, and made nearly 40 pairs of lined curtains. From spring to autumn she filled every room with flower arrangements.

When the Earl of Mar and Kellie died, his grandson offered Kellie for sale to the Lorimers. So, in 1948, the family that had rented the castle almost uninterruptedly for 70 years became the owners. Some restoration of the castle was funded by the Historic Buildings Council, and was completed in 1953. After Mary's death in 1970, Kellie was bought by the National Trust for Scotland. Hew Lorimer continued to live there and the castle was open to the public during the summer.

Some of the contents were purchased by the Trust with a government grant of £10,000, and the rest remained on loan from the Lorimers. In 1998 the Trust was able to buy a third of Sir Robert Lorimer's collection, inherited by Mary, with the aid of grants from the Heritage Lottery Fund and support from the National Museums Purchase Fund. Some remaining items were bought when they came up for auction in Edinburgh in 2003.

Top: Portrait by John Henry of his mother Hannah

Above: Mary Lorimer in the 1940s

Hew Lorimer

Hew Lorimer, one of twentieth-century Scotland's outstanding sculptors, was born in 1907. Kellie, where he lived and worked for over 50 years, was a major influence on his art, as it had been on that of his father Robert and his uncle John Henry.

The young Hew saw Scottish sculptors at work on his father's National War Memorial in Edinburgh Castle, and this probably affected his choice of career.

The great Romanesque and early Gothic monuments of continental Europe remained a central inspiration throughout his life, as did his study with the English sculptor Eric Gill. Both contributed to his spiritual approach to art and to his adoption of the demanding technique of carving directly on to stone.

Hew's best-known works are the Seven Allegorical Figures on the façade of the National Library of Scotland in Edinburgh (this photograph shows him at work on these) and Our Lady of the Isles on the island of South Uist.

Kellie was the scene of local celebrations marking King George V's coronation in 1910. A commemorative postcard shows that cock-fighting was still a popular 'sport' at this time

The Castle

The classic elements of Scottish Renaissance architecture are all here at Kellie – a building of variegated local sandstone that rises dramatically from the garden sheer to the eaves; crowstepped gables, dormer windows, string courses, corbelling, moulded chimney copes; and an enchanting little Renaissance window and a quaint carved gargoyle for good measure. The original roofing of Arbroath stone tiles has had to be entirely replaced, over the past 100 years, by Ballachulish slates.

The castle now takes the form of a T, the stem of which runs east and west; the crossbar north and south. At the northern, southern and eastern extremities of the T stand towers of different dates. The north-west tower is the oldest and the first ten feet or so of walls and stairs may be as early as the fourteenth century. The ground and first-floor chambers are stone-vaulted and therefore certainly of fifteenth-century date. The next oldest portion of the castle, a five-storey tower, stands about 50 ft east of the north-west tower. Nothing is known of what kind of buildings, if any, or what form of courtyard originally connected these two towers.

It is thought that the fourth Lord Oliphant added two upper floors to the east tower in 1573. By 1606 his grandson, the fifth Lord Oliphant, had completed a third tower to the south-west and embellished the older north-west tower with angle turrets to match the new one. He also remodelled the central portion of the castle, extended it with dormer windows and emblazoned its exterior with Oliphant insignia. At this time the external walls would have been harled (roughcast) and limewashed, making the castle a creamy-white colour and looking very different from its appearance today. Remnants of this harling have recently been discovered.

Kellie Castle floor plan

GROUND FLOOR

Private
NORTH-WEST TOWER
NTS Shop
Old Kitchen (now Tearoom)
Tearoom
Office
SOUTH-WEST TOWER
EAST TOWER
Entrance

FIRST FLOOR

Chapel
1950s Kitchen
Drawing Room
Dining Room
Library

SECOND FLOOR

Private
Bathroom
Professor's Room
Earl's Room
Hew Lorimer's Dressing Room
Vine Room
Private
John Henry Lorimer Room

In the south-west tower on the third floor is the Blue Room, and on the fourth floor the Nursery. In the north-west tower on the fourth floor is John Henry Lorimer's Studio (not open to visitors).

The new south-west tower became the castle entrance, providing access to the fashionable suite of apartments above, in the central section, via a new 'scale-and-platt' stair – straight as opposed to the older form of spiral stair. Then a turnpike stair from the first floor led up to the second floor of the central portion – to what is now the Earl's Room – and to the three rooms of the south-west tower, now the John Henry Lorimer Room, the Blue Room and the Nursery.

The north-west and south-west towers are linked across the central portion of the building by a bold false gable with moulded crowsteps. This was possibly carried out by the first Earl of Kellie around 1617.

The three crescent moons of the Oliphants just visible on the pediments of the dormer windows (picture **1**, right), the coat-of-arms of the first Earl of Kellie (**2**), and the inscription over the entrance doorway relating to the Lorimers' restoration work (**3**), identify the three families that inhabited the castle from 1360 to 1970.

Kellie is fortunate to have escaped the substantial additions so often tacked on to Scottish castles and mansion houses. It was abandoned during that part of the nineteenth century when projects of this kind were generally undertaken and Professor Lorimer had neither the means nor the inclination to interfere with the original style of the building.

HOC·DOMICILIUM·CORVIS·ET·BUBONIBUS·EREPTUM
HONESTO·INTER·LABORES·OTIO·CONSECRATUM·EST
A·S· MDCCCLXXVIII· JAL·

Tour of the house

Entrance and staircase

The main door to the castle leads directly to the principal staircase, which may date from the early seventeenth century: its wide stone steps provide a grand and formal approach to the reception rooms on the first floor. The timber panelling that surrounds it mimics the balusters of the great stone cantilevered staircase leading to the King's Apartments in the Palace of Holyroodhouse in Edinburgh.

The landing at the first floor must have been opened up later, with its simple timber railing imitating late Georgian square iron balusters. If you look closely, you can see that the panelling over the entrance door has been made good with discarded shutters from elsewhere.

This is the first of the all-white interiors introduced throughout Kellie by Hew and Mary Lorimer, possibly to replace a dark grey, patches of which survive elsewhere in the castle. In the Lorimers' day, the hooks on the landing would be hung with coats and hats, including Lady Lorimer's straw gardening hats. The elegant stool was copied from a Dutch original by Sir Robert Lorimer, who also collected the tile pictures.

The table on the landing has a rare baroque top in a tortoiseshell parquetry that may be Continental. The Trust introduced the local Pittenweem longcase clock. At the windows Mary Lorimer hung buff damask curtains with large red tassels, originally made for the adjacent Drawing Room. In February 2007, during repairs, fragments of a possibly Jacobean panelling scheme were found over the stair, with wood grained to imitate more expensive hardwoods.

Right: The entrance hall photographed in the days of Hew and Mary Lorimer

The Drawing Room

This room was the Great Hall in the early days of the castle. In 1676 it was fitted up as a great dining room. At first sight it gives the impression of a spacious classical interior, with its richly decorated plaster ceiling and Doric pilasters recalling the contemporary royal apartments at Holyroodhouse. But its irregularities, though skilfully disguised, betray the longer history of Kellie.

Right: A carved alabaster relief, probably Flemish, of c1550. It shows Orpheus taming the beasts with his music

Top: A photograph of 1893 shows how the Lorimers furnished this room informally but artistically, as befitted their holiday home. The professor introduced the dark stain on the floorboards, as a background to the oriental rugs. The Carolean (or Restoration) formality of the room was restored by his sons John Henry and Robert. Evidence of this change in taste can be seen clearly in the Country Life *photograph of 1906 (smaller image)*

The great south-facing sash windows that flood the room with light are the glory of the room, and were cited as models in a building contract for Sir Philip Anstruther's nearby house in 1633. The heraldry of the ceiling, bearing the date 1676, records the marriage of Alexander, the third Earl of Kellie, and his second wife Mary Dalzell, in 1665. The architectural detailing of the timber Doric pilasters is unusually fine, as are the doorcases. This suggests the involvement of the King's Surveyor, Sir William Bruce, who supervised the rebuilding of Holyroodhouse and who in 1665 acquired the estate of Balcaskie, adjoining Kellie.

This room became a Drawing Room about 1800, when the heavily enriched Scottish chimneypiece frieze, depicting the god Mars returning from battle in triumph, was added to the fireplace on the east wall.

Robert Lorimer designed the cartouches (ornamental scrolls) over the chimneypieces bearing his, his brother John Henry's and their mother's monograms: these were carved by the Clow brothers, Lorimer's favourite and most talented carvers, in 1897. The professor's yellow striped paper was torn down and the Wheelers, local craftsmen based at nearby Arncroach, patched what remained of the old panelling and added mouldings to recreate the impression of a panelled interior. A big rectangle of painted canvas was left on the north wall, where Robert believed a tapestry would have hung in the seventeenth century. The third fireplace became a recess for displaying porcelain, finished off with a carved sprig of cherry.

In 1897 John Henry commissioned the artist Phoebe Traquair, a friend of the Lorimer brothers, to fill the large panel over the second fireplace, on the south wall. Tiles imported from Antwerp were set around the stone chimneypiece, one of many throughout the castle that most probably date from the 1676 alterations.

Traquair revealed

Phoebe Anna Traquair worked in jewellery and embroidery as well as mural painting. Robert Lorimer wrote of her: 'I don't think I know anyone who is as sympathetic to me artistically. She's so sane, such a lover of simplicity, and the things that give real lasting pleasure are the simplest things of nature.' John Henry asked her to decorate the panel over the second fireplace with 'a procession of girls following a wee cupid'. The painting is based on Botticelli's *Primavera*.

Hew and Mary Lorimer, who lived here from the mid-1930s, did not admire the panel and had it carefully papered over to complete their all-white look. This allowed it to be revealed again by Albert Cumming of the Stenhouse Conservation Centre and NTS curator Christopher Hartley in 1996, following a popular exhibition of Traquair's work at the Scottish National Portrait Gallery in Edinburgh. The paper was carefully removed with a wooden scalpel to avoid scratching the painted surface.

Traquair was the first woman member of the Royal Scottish Academy and the leading Arts & Crafts artist in Edinburgh, where you can see superb examples of her murals at the St Mary's Episcopal Cathedral Song School, the St Giles' Thistle Chapel and the Mansfield Traquair Centre (formerly the Catholic and Apostolic Church).

After he married, Robert Lorimer took the furniture shown in the 1906 photograph, much of which he had designed himself, to Gibliston, his own country house nearby. John Henry kept his parents' furniture, as a photograph of 1935 records but, following his death in 1936, this was all dispersed in a sale at the castle, as directed in his Will. So Robert's son Hew and his wife Mary had to refurnish this room from scratch when they moved into Kellie.

They were helped by Hew having inherited from his father a very fine collection of antique furniture, including the Jacobean draw-leaf table and the two Dutch oyster parquetry cabinets, as well as the pieces Robert designed himself. Most of this had been used in Sir Robert and Lady Lorimer's drawing room at 54 Melville Street, Edinburgh, including the curvaceous chest of drawers with marble top and the Louis XV-style oak settee, copied from an original owned by John Henry. The walnut marble-topped bookcase in the Louis XV style, with its silvered door handles, was originally paired with a secrétaire or writing desk, but this went elsewhere.

In 2003 the Trust was able to buy back Lady Lorimer's tambour-fronted music cabinet which Sir Robert had converted into a showcase for his *objets d'art*, many of which are still displayed within it, including several pieces from his collection of shagreen (animal or sharkskin) boxes. The pair of elaborately shaped gilt and bevelled mirrors carved with birds, designed by Robert, somehow escaped the sale of his collections stipulated in John Henry's Will. The portraits and sculpture were also inherited from Robert and John Henry.

In contrast to these glamorous furnishings Mary had to harmonise a rather rum collection of make-do-and-mend seat furniture, with loose covers whose colours were chosen with an artist's eye. The cut velvet curtains were among her final contributions.

From top of page: The walnut bookcase and its door handle; Lady Lorimer's cabinet; and part of the collection displayed in it

The Piano

The fortepiano was made about 1825 by the celebrated Stodart family of piano makers. Robert Stodart, who founded the firm, was the grandfather of Professor Lorimer's wife Hannah. His portrait – a copy of the original by Henry Raeburn – hangs in this room. A marquetry panel inset in the instrument's lid records that the company was patronised by the royal family. The piano was restored by Rhodes and Jones of Burntisland in 1974. Hew Lorimer organised many concerts in this room, including one in 1978 featuring the piano music of Schubert, to commemorate the 150th anniversary of the composer's death.

The Chapel

This small vaulted room probably dates from the late fifteenth or early sixteenth century and was the High Hall of the original tower house. When Hew and Mary Lorimer became Roman Catholics they converted it into a small family chapel. The small harmonium and the prayer chairs were designed by Robert Lorimer. The two oil paintings are copies by John Henry Lorimer, after paintings by Italian old masters Bellini and Tiepolo. The stone carving in the alcove is by Antony Foster, who was working with Eric Gill when Hew was a student there.

The Dining Room

This was the second room in the 'great apartment' sequence of rooms favoured in the seventeenth century. It would originally have been the 'Withdrawing Room', where the laird and his family 'withdrew' from the bustle of the Great Hall (now the Drawing Room) next door, and is of much earlier origin than its present decoration. It continues the look of the preceding room, with a similar plaster ceiling and matching doors and doorcases. All three generations of the Lorimers at Kellie used this room as their Dining Room, as it is conveniently connected by a spiral stair to the original kitchen on the floor below.

The room's distinctive character derives from the Italianate painted panels with their lively scenes of palaces, terraced gardens, castles and seascapes, which have few parallels in Scotland. If you look closely at the panel on the left flank of the right-hand window, you can see the 'ghost' of an earlier simpler decorative scheme. It seems sensible, although its dating is not known, to connect these outstanding panels with the ceiling on the floor above, as part of the 1676 modernisation in the most up-to-the-minute fashion of the royal Palace of Holyroodhouse.

The poor condition of the panels reflects Kellie's chequered history – they were saved from total decay in the nick of time by Professor Lorimer. John Henry replaced the missing areas of the scheme with modern panels in a similar spirit – you can readily identify his replacements on the press (cupboard) doors below the north window and on the south-west door that leads back into the Drawing Room.

The old kitchen photographed in the 1970s. It is now the tearoom

Hew and Mary decorated this room in earth tones to complement the all-important decorative paintings which, as in the Drawing Room, must originally have surrounded panels designed to accommodate tapestries. They had only one tapestry, which they hung on the east wall of this room.

A lively French armoire or cupboard filled the north wall and the early medieval feeling of the room was followed through in a collection of Gothic sculpture and old oak. A wrought-iron circular chandelier hung above Hew and Mary's circular table. Mary hung the simplest brown plaid single curtains at the long windows to tone with and show as much of the decorative painting as possible, while the high window was curtained in chenille, picking up the colour of the copperware displayed on its sill.

Mary's brother, the architect Henry Wylie, transformed the original adjacent pantry into an innovative fitted modern kitchen, with red formica worktops. An efficient serving hatch below the high north window connects it with the Dining Room. Previously, Mary and Hew had used the nineteenth-century kitchen on the floor below, but this new arrangement was better suited to life after the Second World War, when there were no longer staff to fetch and carry.

Top: Hew and Mary Lorimer's only tapestry, depicting Europa and the bull, was woven in Brussels in the late sixteenth century: it was photographed by Country Life in 1962. Its patchwork borders had perhaps made it affordable, at a time when tapestries were highly valued by collectors and very expensive. The tapestry was cleaned and restored in 1986 by Linda Eaton of the Scottish Museums Council

The Library

In spite of its diminutive size, this room is of major importance in the development of interior decoration in Scotland. The *Accounts of the Masters of Works for Building and Repairing Royal Palaces and Castles*, the Scottish Office of Works' records of that period, tells us that in June 1617 moulds were delivered to the 'plaisterers from Kellie'. This may therefore be the first room in Scotland where plaster decoration was used, in the London manner, in preference to the painted beams and boarded ceilings that were still generally fashionable. When James VI visited Scotland in 1617, his apartments in Edinburgh Castle had just been redecorated with similar plasterwork and this new fashion was then imitated in many other great houses, such as Glamis and Craigievar.

Here, the date '1617' and the monogram 'T V F' for Thomas Viscount Fentoun, his title before being created the first Earl of Kellie, are incorporated in the ceiling. As one of James VI and I's Scottish courtiers in London, Thomas would have been familiar with this kind of interior decoration and it may be that this room was created in anticipation of a royal visit.

This room, which the Lorimers always had painted white, was repaired in 1878 to provide a study for Professor Lorimer. The small bookcase with the glazed top contains *The Red Book of Kellie*, his extensive research into the history of the castle. The chimneypiece incorporates a copy, by Hannah Lorimer, of Raeburn's portrait of the Scottish philosopher Thomas Reid. In Hew and Mary's time it became an attractive family sitting room, more readily warmed than the larger rooms of the castle.

When Kellie was acquired by the National Trust for Scotland in 1970, after Mary's death, Hew retreated to the rooms in the south-east tower and, as he grew older, this room became his study in preference to the attic over his studio. Happily Mary's curtains survive, but without their pelmet. The Lorimer family lent back Hew's books in 2001.

Above: Mary Lorimer's decoration of the Library was recorded by this Country Life *photograph in 1962*

Below: Fragment of Renaissance tapestry found at Kellie

In 2007 a showcase was added to display one of Kellie's most precious relics, a fragment of *mille-fleurs* tapestry depicting strawberry fruits and flowers on a black ground. This style of tapestry was characteristic of late fifteenth- and early sixteenth-century France. The fragment was found, together with the lace-making tools displayed alongside, under the floor of the room above during repairs, as Hew's inscription on the box records. It gives a vivid impression of how colourful the interiors of Kellie may have been in their prime.

An exceptionally fine inlaid chest of drawers from Hew's collection, designed by the young Robert Lorimer in his early Arts & Crafts manner, is also shown in this room.

The South-West Tower Rooms

These light and sunny rooms may originally have been intended as a guest suite. Hew and Mary assigned the rooms to their three children. They are connected by a circular stair, which has recently been repainted in its original red.

Above: The Professor's Grandchildren by John Henry Lorimer shows the children looking out of a window in the castle

Below: This door in the Nursery probably dates from 1617

Below right: A detail of the Nursery screen decorated with Edwardian 'scraps'

The John Henry Lorimer Room

This was the bedroom of Robin, Hew and Mary's elder son. In 1972, when the National Trust for Scotland first opened Kellie to visitors, this room was dedicated to commemorating Sir Robert Lorimer. In 2005, however, it was felt that the architect's reputation had been successfully re-established, while his artist brother, John Henry Lorimer, was still less known. The Trust had been given, and had purchased, a number of works by the artist and the Scottish National Portrait Gallery had kindly lent their portraits of his mother and father. The impetus for creating the present room was the loan of two paintings from the Edinburgh Astronomical Society, to which the artist left his estate.

The room was painted a sympathetic grey because John Henry's paintings do not seem comfortable on the prevailing Kellie white, and this colour reflects the greyish tone on the panelling of his studio at the very top of the north-west tower. Unfortunately, although the studio remains much as John Henry left it, it cannot be shown to visitors because of the hazardous, irregular steps of the north spiral stair. This stair made it difficult for the artist to get his larger canvasses up and down, and a casement window was built into the room so that they could be lowered down the outside wall on ropes.

The Nursery

This room, which belonged to Henry, Hew and Mary's younger son, has the tongue-and-groove pine linings that are typical of the professor's and the Earl's roof repairs in 1878, and was originally unpainted. As you enter, the door looks prosaic enough, but its inside face reveals fine Jacobean decoration and fretted hinges that indicate it may be of the same period as the 1617 plasterwork of the Library. The room was redecorated in 1981 to display a collection of nursery furnishings, donated by the NTS East Fife Members' Centre to commemorate the 50th anniversary of the Trust.

The Blue Room

This room has early eighteenth-century panelling but the grate is later, and is typical of those installed by the professor and his sons, with ironwork by the local Arncroach ironworker and blacksmith, James Bennet. This room was decorated by Mary for her daughter Monica, and it was one of her most fully worked-out schemes. The panelling was painted blue and both the windows and the tester bed, with its deep blue velvet bow, were hung with white lightly patterned cobwebby voile curtains with deep gathered valances, backed by a matching blue lining.

A small desk was also painted blue but the dressing table was draped in white to match the curtains. A set of delicate painted Gothic chairs, reputedly from Crawford Priory, were well matched to the fragility and lightness of Mary's imaginative scheme. The ornaments continued the blue theme or added fresh colours like pink, picking up the colour wash of the grate. With a thoroughness that reveals the seriousness of her decoration, Mary chose only blue-bound books for the shelves.

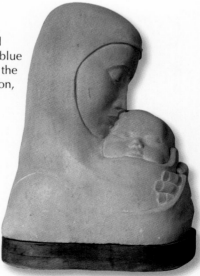

Above left: The oak cradle, carved with a guardian angel and a pelican, was designed by Robert Lorimer for his children. Above right: The Blue Room as Mary Lorimer decorated it, in a Country Life *photograph of 1962*

Right: Mother and Child, *by the Scottish sculptor Thomas Whalen, who studied under the same tutor as Hew Lorimer*

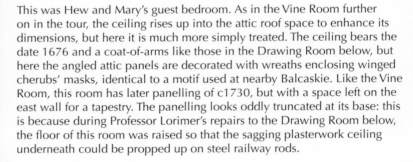

Top left: The Earl's Room in Hew and Mary Lorimer's time, photographed in 1962, and (right) today

The Earl's Room

This was Hew and Mary's guest bedroom. As in the Vine Room further on in the tour, the ceiling rises up into the attic roof space to enhance its dimensions, but here it is much more simply treated. The ceiling bears the date 1676 and a coat-of-arms like those in the Drawing Room below, but here the angled attic panels are decorated with wreaths enclosing winged cherubs' masks, identical to a motif used at nearby Balcaskie. Like the Vine Room, this room has later panelling of c1730, but with a space left on the east wall for a tapestry. The panelling looks oddly truncated at its base: this is because during Professor Lorimer's repairs to the Drawing Room below, the floor of this room was raised so that the sagging plasterwork ceiling underneath could be propped up on steel railway rods.

The panelling was painted white, as throughout the castle, and the tapestry panel was filled with a modern printed chintz, with feathers enclosed by yellow-and-white wreaths tied with tasselled strings, reflecting those on the ceiling above. Clearly, as so often in Mary's post-war make-do-and-mend projects, there was not quite enough of the chintz, so she framed the panel in matching velvet, which was probably second-hand.

An old brass bed was pressed into service but given a contemporary feel with lace hangings over a yellow ground to match the colours in the chintz. A canopy-type tester was improvised from half of a circular gilt picture frame (the other half remains in the attics). There were just enough scraps of the chintz left over to give a Dior 'New Look' treatment to the oval Queen Anne stool. An old Regency sofa became a day-bed under the plush valance, and a Georgian card table became a writing table. New chintz curtains were made for this room in 1996 but Mary's bed hangings and dressing table cover survived and her missing decorations have been recreated.

The Professor's Room

This room was a rather utilitarian bathroom used by Hew and Mary's children, who remember it as icy cold. In 1976 Esther Chalmers, the professor's granddaughter, funded its transformation into a family room commemorating him. At the same time it was redecorated to create a typically Victorian interior – not entirely appropriate at Kellie, where the Lorimers' taste had never been typical. In 2007 John Henry's portrait of his father was moved to the John Henry Lorimer Room, and the decoration was simplified to display more sympathetically a range of Lorimer family memorabilia, much of it both presented and generously loaned by William Lorimer, Hew's nephew.

Hew's Dressing Room and the Pink Bathroom

This room was divided by Henry Wylie in 1957 to create a new bathroom for Hew and Mary at its north end and a new window had to be punched through the north façade to light it. The pink paper, contrasting the lives of a wild and a caged bird, looks Parisian but was in fact made by Crown, the renowned English firm. Mary followed this through with a china dove on the lavatory cistern, a French garden chair, and her favourite voile curtains.

Hew's room is now dominated by a large late Georgian wardrobe. Mary chose to use William Morris's 'willow bough' wallpaper here, a rather pioneering Morris Revival experiment. The dressing table is from Professor Lorimer's house in Bruntsfield, Edinburgh. Mary's portrait of her daughter Monica has always hung in this room: it has now been joined by small-scale cabinet pictures and watercolours by John Henry Lorimer, many of which have been presented to the National Trust for Scotland.

Above: Mary Lorimer's unfinished portrait of her daughter Monica, aged six; her elegant choice of bathroom wallpaper

The Vine Room

This is the most celebrated interior at Kellie. Although situated at the top of the house, there is every reason to assume it was intended as the state bedroom in the suite of great apartments. It was connected by the circular stair to the Dining Room (later the Drawing Room) and Withdrawing Room (later the Dining Room) below. As on the south-west stair, the top landing of this stair has a fine wooden balustrade that may date from the 1617 alterations – such early woodwork is exceptionally rare in Scotland and a particularly miraculous survival at Kellie.

The room emulates the King's Bedroom at the Palace of Holyroodhouse in Edinburgh, the centrepiece of Charles II and Sir William Bruce's design. The ceiling painting is a smaller version by Jacob de Witt, Charles II's own painter, of his illusionist ceiling at Holyroodhouse, showing Hercules being received onto Mount Olympus by Mercury. It is on canvas, and it is possible that de Witt painted it in his Edinburgh studio, and would not necessarily have visited Kellie. The painting has a romantic and eventful history. The daughter of the eleventh Earl of Kellie took it to her new home in Ireland in 1830. But in December 1916 the fourteenth Earl traced it and took advantage of 'a chance that might not recur' to buy it for £100 and repatriate it to Kellie.

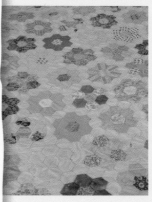

The attic roof space was incorporated in the room to give it suitably impressive dimensions. This created large panels which the plasterers filled with engagingly naturalistic vines, from which the room takes its name, though it has recently been suggested that the fruit depicted may be hops (which used to be stuffed in pillows to encourage sleep). The plasterwork was in a perilous state when Kellie was rescued by Professor Lorimer, who employed local plasterers Williamsons of Pittenweem to replace the entire north panel by creating a cast from the undamaged south panel.

Robert Lorimer designed a canopied tester bed with crewelwork embroidery in wool on linen for this room. It was supported on simple wooden brackets, so that the splendid ceiling was not obscured from the occupants of the bed. These hangings, embroidered by Robert's sister Louise and the local postmistress, were subsequently presented to the National Museums of Scotland. Hew and Mary inherited only the wooden brackets, still *in situ,* and Mary created the present bed around a late Gothic gilded carving of the Virgin and Child. She incorporated light voile curtains and a Victorian patchwork quilt in the purplish tones she chose for this room.

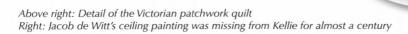

Above right: Detail of the Victorian patchwork quilt
Right: Jacob de Witt's ceiling painting was missing from Kellie for almost a century

Right: This Country Life *photograph of 1906 shows Robert Lorimer's bed hangings in the Vine Room, and the ceiling before the de Witt painting was replaced in 1916*

Below: Mary Lorimer's furnishings in a Country Life *photograph of 1962*

Matching curtains, with the same bobble fringe, were made for the north window but the south windows had the most elaborate 'New Look' curtains, which recall a Dior summer dress of the 1950s. These had disintegrated in the sunlight by the time the Trust took over Kellie. We are recreating Mary's curtains as well as reinstating her patchwork of floor coverings – white wool carpets and ethnic embroidered rugs, eked out with sheepskin rugs.

The bedroom has a fine French armoire for a wardrobe, and a handsome early Robert Lorimer chest of drawers. Mary's dressing table cover and the loose cover of her daybed with its lace overlays have happily survived. Although done with simple materials and on a tight budget, the verve of Mary's decoration, with its period prints of Redouté roses, responds to the spirit of the lively plasterwork above.

Caring for the collections

As you walk around the castle you will see little light-grey boxes, strategically placed, showing relative humidity and temperature readings in each room. Additionally, sensors in vulnerable areas will record light levels. This data is recorded twenty-four hours a day and 365 days a year, and is vital to enable us to prevent environmental damage to the collections at Kellie. The contents of the castle are also protected by a rigorous housekeeping routine. If any repairs are needed, we call in conservators who are specialists in their field.

The Garden

The garden at Kellie is a magical place – a 'secret garden' entered through a door in the high stone wall. It entices you in to enjoy the sweet-smelling old-fashioned roses, the herbaceous borders packed with colourful flowers, the neat rows of well-tended vegetables and the songs of birds in the old apple trees. Despite changes in the planting schemes and the laying of lawns in the 1950s, Kellie remains a traditional Scottish walled garden, with fruit, flowers and vegetables all grown together. An informal cottage-garden style of planting is still very much in evidence, enclosed by box hedging that defines the early seventeenth-century formal path network. The entire garden is cultivated using organic methods.

History of the garden

Walled gardens, which originated in Renaissance Italy, were quickly adopted by garden designers in northern Europe, and were particularly favoured in Scotland, since they provided effective shelter from a harsh climate. The walled garden at Kellie was designed around 400 years ago, when the castle was enlarged by the fifth Lord Oliphant. It is probable that an earlier walled garden existed at Kellie, but there are no records to show how it looked.

Sir Thomas Erskine, who was made the first Earl of Kellie in 1619, was able to recreate elements of other European gardens in this walled environment by using plants such as box and yew. It is probable that he even grew some of the delicate plants found in warmer climates, such as figs and peaches, with the assistance of the heat-retaining walls. Unfortunately little detail is known about this early garden: before the Lorimers arrived at Kellie, the garden records were moved to Cambo House, where they were later destroyed in a fire.

An engraving of 1570 by the Flemish artist Hans Bol, showing a northern European walled garden

It would be reasonable to assume that the renowned seventeenth-century architect Sir William Bruce, who was a neighbour and friend of Alexander, the third Earl, influenced the design of the garden, as well as elements of the house. It had become fashionable to interpret the house and garden as an entity, and Bruce planned his home, Balcaskie, so that the view and landscape were an integral part of the grand design. The garden at Kellie, though planned in relation to the house, was a more modest, enclosed garden of the traditional Scottish type: formal in layout, and containing an orchard, ornamentals, vegetables, herbs and fruits within sturdy protective walls.

The seventeenth-century supermarket

In its early days the garden at Kellie was particularly important as the 'supermarket' of its time, providing the household with all the fresh fruit and vegetables it needed. Surplus produce was kept for the lean winter months, either by storing it in pits in the ground, or by preserving it in the castle kitchens. Honey – an important sweetener before sugar became widely available – was gathered from the bee skeps (wickerwork hives) that sat in the bee boles in the old stone walls. There were originally six of these: three have been filled in, but three remain open and still contain the traditional skeps.

The Kellie household would also once have relied for food and other supplies on the many farms in the estate, which originally extended to 1,100 acres.

Above, from top: The armillary sphere sundial, focus of the central walkway; a 1905 photograph of the statue of Cupid in Robert Lorimer's 'Secret Garden'; Clematis 'Comtesse de Bouchaud'

The fact that Kellie was unoccupied for much of the nineteenth century was no less beneficial to the garden than it was to the house – they both escaped many 'improvements', which often included the removal of the utilitarian walled garden away from the house and its replacement by landscaped parkland with trees.

However, decades of neglect also affected the garden as much as the house. When Professor Lorimer discovered Kellie in the 1870s, his daughter Louise wrote of the state of the garden: 'still encircled by a tumbledown wall, [it] was a wilderness of neglected gooseberry bushes, gnarled apple trees and old-world roses, which struggled through the weeds, summer after summer, with a sweet persistence'. The Lorimers set to work.

They organised for cuttings to be taken from the overgrown shrubs and plants, and improved on the existing design, probably with a strong input from the young Robert. They created a central grass walkway bordered by hollyhocks and intersected by a path edged with *Rosa mundi* hedges. At the intersection, they placed a sundial in the form of an armillary sphere – a skeleton sphere made up of hoops, showing the motions of the celestial bodies. In 1900 they added the beautiful stone summerhouse, with its unusual bird-like creature perched on the rooftop – one of Robert's hallmarks.

Two small corner gardens were added: Robin's Corner and the Yew Enclosure (usually referred to as the Secret Garden). These 'gardens within gardens' often appear in Sir Robert Lorimer's later work, and were characteristic features of the Edwardian gardens designed by his contemporaries and friends such as William Robinson and Gertrude Jekyll.

The planting and propagating of plants for the garden was something that most of the Lorimer family took part in. Letters written by the professor's wife Hannah and by her daughters show their enormous enthusiasm for the garden. Louise, in particular, became quite an expert. For 25 years she divided her time between looking after the garden and caring for her mother. In an essay entitled 'The Final Choice', she considered which rose she would keep if she were deprived of all but one and, after itemising all the varieties in the Kellie garden, finally settled on 'the Old Blush, the common China'. This is a fascinating record of the roses that the Lorimers grew here, many of which are still grown today.

'The ideal of what a Scotch gentleman's home ought to be – the house... looks onto a garden that has a quite different sort of charm from the park outside, a garden that is an intentional and deliberate piece of careful design... but that becomes less trim as it gets further from the house, and then naturally and gradually marries with the demesne that lies beyond.'

Robert Lorimer, in 'On Scottish Gardens', Architectural Review November 1899

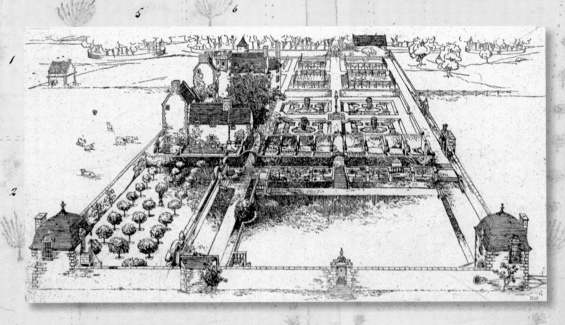

Above: Robert Lorimer's 1892 design for the gardens at Earlshall, Fife

Background: Lorimer's first design for a garden at Kellie, drawn in 1880, when he was sixteen

The Scottish pleasaunce

'A garden is a sort of sanctuary, a chamber roofed by heaven ...
The garden is a little pleasaunce of the soul, by whose wicket the
world can be shut out from us.'

Robert Lorimer, in 'On Scottish Gardens', Architectural Review *November 1899*

When the Lorimers revived the garden at Kellie, they respected its character. It had retained many of the features of the 'pleasaunce', the medieval enclosed garden attached to a castle or large house, dedicated to pleasure and recreation, and designed to delight all the senses. Walled gardens had survived more in Scotland than in England because they were better suited to the wilder climate and terrain and the more modest means of the landowners. The living tradition of the Scottish pleasaunce, with its massive walls, parterres, summerhouses, wall planting and recesses for flowers, became a major inspiration for British garden architects of the 1890s. Robert Lorimer's designs for the gardens at Earlshall, in Fife, show him creating a typical 'pleasaunce', and putting into practice ideas that he first tried out at Kellie.

Kellie Castle, Garden 1880.

After the death of Hannah Lorimer, her son John Henry took on the lease of Kellie. When he died in 1936, the castle was once more without a tenant and the garden fell into neglect again. It was only when Hew and Mary Lorimer took on the tenancy in 1937 that the garden was rescued. They brought back the old gardener, Jim Dowie, who was 70 years old by this time. In Hew's words: 'This Herculean task he undertook single-handed on one condition, that if he tackled the forking and the digging involved in cleansing the soil, someone else (and it could be no one but me) should do the barrowing. We worked with two barrows and he filled and I emptied until the spring came.'

In the 1950s, with a smaller family in the house, and the cost of labour rising, it became less practical to have so much of the garden under vegetable cultivation. Vegetable production was restricted to the early beds along the south-facing north wall.

Respecting the spirit of the place

When the National Trust for Scotland took over responsibility for Kellie in 1970, the garden was again somewhat neglected. Restoration is still continuing. In recent years, the vegetable and fruit borders below the north-facing walls have been reclaimed from the lawns by the garden entrance. These now support a rhubarb collection with over 24 edible varieties, as well as other vegetables and shade-tolerant fruits – blackberry, redcurrant, gooseberry and acid cherry, which are grown on the north wall. A collection of old apple varieties now fills the orchard and the south, east and west walls of the garden, along with trained forms of pear and plum. Many old potato varieties are also grown in the garden.

Crucial to the Trust's management of the garden is the principle that we should remain true to the 'spirit of the place', without preserving it in aspic. Over its lifetime the garden has evolved, and new plants have been introduced by its various owners and tenants: the Trust's management respects this history. We have changed the original planting on the central walkway without destroying the original concept. There once was an avenue of hollyhocks here, which succumbed to rust. Rather than spraying hollyhocks with chemicals each year, we decided to plant delphiniums instead, with the dominant feature of catmint (Nepeta x faassenii) along the front. Jacobite roses (Rosa x alba 'Alba Maxima') arch out of wrought-iron hoops all the way down the border and, with their delicate white blooms, make a wonderful contrast to the predominantly blue avenue. Recently, Robin's Corner has been replanted with old roses and lilies that are all white, a contrast to the luxuriant herbaceous planting everywhere around. This corner, enclosed by a green trellis fence topped by white cones, is now echoed by a similar area in the opposite corner of the garden, where an old shed once stood, providing a pleasantly shaded seating area.

Above, from top: Two photographs of the 1940s showing Hew Lorimer in the garden, and the vegetable plot; Cardoon (Cynara cardunculus); forget-me-not (Myosotis alpestris) with Nepeta x faassenii

Cultivation

Methods used throughout the history of the garden are still favoured today by Trust staff. Apples, pears, peaches, figs, plums and cherries are trained in the traditional forms of cordon, fan and espalier, to maximise fruit production in the allotted space (**1**) and (**2**). Varieties of apple such as the bramley, pear and plum that grow better as free-standing specimens are grown in the orchard, or on the other lawns.

Historically, fruits were selected to provide a long season. Rhubarb was important, particularly by Victorian times, as an early 'fruit' for desserts, although strictly speaking it is a vegetable. The forcing pots we use in the garden today would also have been used in the past to extend the picking season, by producing early tender shoots (**3**).

Traditional techniques

1

3

2

4

We also use centuries-old techniques of extending the growing season for vegetables. The partly shaded borders below the north-facing wall slow down a crop, providing later vegetables, while the warm south-facing borders that heat up quickly in the spring sunshine produce early crops, sometimes followed by a second crop of something else. Victorian lantern cloches are put in position early to provide the crop with extra protection from late frosts, wind and rain (**4**).

Storage

Apples were stored at Kellie through most of the winter and into spring. The Lorimer family used the old wine cellar as an apple store, as it provided the constant, cool, yet frost-free temperatures required to keep apples successfully. Now we use the old wood shed at Kellie – and it might just have been a purpose-built Victorian apple store, since it was built in stone, onto the north side of a stone wall, and so has a constant temperature. The only merit it lacks is good ventilation. We also use carrot clamps and potato pits, traditional techniques for storing winter vegetables.

COVNTRY HOMES · GARDENS OLD · & NEW KELLIE CASTLE, FIFE . . . THE RESIDENCE OF MRS. LORIMER.

Organic Kellie

The garden and estate have been managed organically since 1990. The Trust uses only natural methods to improve growth and control pests – one of the biggest challenges of organic gardening.

At Kellie, the soil not only acts as an anchor for plant roots, but also as a slow-release repository of nutrients, providing them when the plant needs them. Some nutrients are leached out of the soil by rainwater: to counteract this, we add to the soil bulky organic matter, which contains bacteria that gradually break it down and decompose it. Or we add 'green manure' to patches of soil between plantings: the manure takes up the nutrients in the soil and prevents their leaching. It is then simply dug back into the soil before the area is needed for the next crop, where it breaks down, releasing all those nutrients slowly back into the soil. Many plants can be used as a green manure – we often use ryegrass, clover or tares.

Clay is inherently rich in plant nutrients which are slowly released as the clay weathers. At Kellie, the soil has a very low clay content, so adding organic matter is very important to maintain fertility. However, our soil is also high in sand content, which allows the soil to warm up more quickly in the spring, creating a longer growing season. The same piece of ground will often yield two and sometimes three crops a year.

By growing a wide range of plant types together, rather than having large beds of the same crop or ornamental plant, which would attract a particular pest, we reduce the severity of pest attack. Some pests, such as the cabbage white butterfly, find their host plant by sight, so if our cabbages are dotted among a clump of nasturtiums they often go unnoticed by the butterfly (**1**).

Many birds help to control pests and, by providing bird feeders all year round, we host many more of the various species than would normally be present in a garden of this size. We also use cultural control methods, such as barriers, to prevent crawling insects climbing trees to attack fruits; or pheromone traps, which use the scent released by a female insect to attract and capture pests (**2**).

Companion planting has become one of our main lines of defence in the garden. Certain plants benefit each other when planted together: their roots or foliage secrete substances that encourage growth in other plants; or their scent disguises that from a neighbouring plant, confusing pests. The *Allium* family (onions, chives, leeks, garlic, etc) are very powerful natural fungicides and protect other plants grown beside them from fungal diseases. For this reason, onions are often grown at Kellie next to strawberries and the ornamental *Allium* beside roses (**3**).

We grow new as well as 'heritage' varieties: it is important in an organic garden where no chemicals are used to grow modern varieties that have been bred for their resistance to disease or pests. Many modern vegetable varieties are much more palatable than their Victorian counterparts. However, the opposite is true of fruit crops – in general the older varieties have the best flavours.

Companion planting tips

1 Plant borage *(Borago officinalis)* or pot marigold *(Calendula officinalis)* next to beans to act as a decoy. They will attract blackfly away from French, runner and broad beans.

2 Plant poached egg plants *(Limnanthes douglasii)* between vegetables to attract hoverflies. These insects will then devour any aphids they find on nearby vegetables.

3 Plant nasturtiums *(Tropaeolum majus)* around or between brassica plants (cabbages, broccoli, etc). They encourage vigour in these plants and also act as a decoy plant. Aphids much prefer nasturtiums to brassicas.

4 Plant French marigolds *(Tagetes patula)* close to plants that are susceptible to attack from nematodes (parasitic worms). Marigolds inhibit nematodes in the root region.

Learning in the garden

The garden plays an important part in the Trust's education programme. The Education Room is linked to the garden, where the diversity of species cultivated organically provides a rich resource for nature study or for art activities. The Trust organises 'Living History' tours that give children of all ages an insight into life at a Scottish house and garden during wartime in the 1940s. They learn how the garden would have been run; the role of women in producing food in the garden; what sort of foods were eaten, and how they were cooked or preserved.

In 2005 we launched the Organic Gardening Studentship programme at Kellie Castle, to equip a student with an academic horticulture qualification with the practical skills to manage an organic garden. The course is linked with the Trust's School of Practical Gardening at Threave, and with the Henry Doubleday Research Association's heritage seed programme, by growing a selection of its old and sometimes very rare vegetable varieties, once widely cultivated in Britain's great gardens but now no longer available.

The Wider Estate

Early maps of Kellie, for example Roy's military survey (1747-55), (below left) and John Ainslie's map of 1775 (below right), show a formal avenue flanked by trees leading right up to the front of the castle. Sometime between 1801 and 1828 the current driveway was adopted, and all that remains of the original avenue are the two great specimen sycamores on the front lawn of the castle, which must be around 300 years old. The estate of Kellie originally extended to hundreds of acres. Over the centuries, land was sold off or gambled away, until it was reduced to the humble estate of today – approximately 7.24 hectares (17 acres) of parkland, meadow and woods.

Paths through the estate

Beginning at the car park, take the meandering path through Kellie Wood, to the west of the estate, a beautiful place to walk. The path follows the burn upstream, past the large pond that is now surrounded by ferns and semi-natural planting. A bridge takes you across to the castle from the top of the pond or you can follow the path to the left, through the children's adventure playground and over another bridge further upstream, where the woodland path meanders along the north side of the walled garden. Fine views of the hill Kellie Law can be enjoyed from this section of path before you emerge at the meadow, after passing the bird hide. Close-mown paths take you through the meadow back to the front of the castle, or in the other direction off the estate boundary towards Kellie Law.

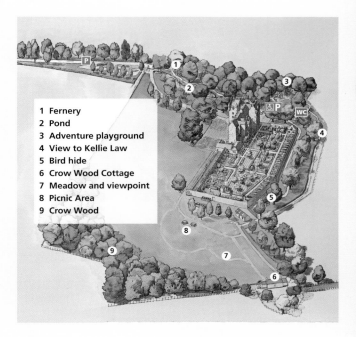

1 Fernery
2 Pond
3 Adventure playground
4 View to Kellie Law
5 Bird hide
6 Crow Wood Cottage
7 Meadow and viewpoint
8 Picnic Area
9 Crow Wood

Woodland

Trees are an important part of Kellie's character, and mark its boundaries with the surrounding arable farmland. Sadly, Dutch elm disease has taken its toll, but sycamore, beech, oak, ash, willow, yew, holly, hawthorn and elder still flourish here. Elder often naturalises in areas once used as middens or dumps by the gardeners or household of Kellie – areas rich in nitrogen.

Yew trees, like the one next to the bird hide, are believed to be among the longest living organisms. There is a saying that they take 'a thousand years to grow, a thousand years to die', but many trees are in fact even older than this. It is difficult to assess their age accurately because the trunks usually become hollow after about 500 years. Yew is poisonous, and has been known to be fatal to humans. You will sometimes see birds eating the berries, but they eat only the red flesh and not the seeds, the most poisonous part.

In early spring drifts of snowdrops and aconites line the woodland walks and the pond, followed by daffodils, especially along the driveway to the castle. In May, the beautiful white flowers of wild garlic carpet the woods, with clumps of bluebells peeping through. Ferns and red campions follow, along with a great drift of balsam near the adventure playground. We keep an eye on the balsam, as it is a highly invasive plant in the wild. The fernery, which was planted in an old log pile by the path in the woods, contains many different species of fern. You will also see interesting mosses here and, in winter, fascinating types of fungi.

Below: The Long Shadows: Woodland Scene at Kellie *by John Henry Lorimer*

The pond

Robert Lorimer wrote to his sister Alice on 12 March 1882: 'The lake in the glen is a great improvement but will look much nicer than it does at present when the banks which are now just red earth are grown with ferns, grass, etc.' His letter indicates that the Lorimers were designing the pond around this time: there is no record of its existence on earlier maps. The pond is fed by Kellie Burn, and provides a habitat for frogs, ducks and an occasional heron. Watch out for mink, a visitor to the pond and burn – an introduced species that is a deadly enemy to much of the native wildlife.

In winter the bright red stems of the dogwood *(Cornus alba* 'Sibirica'*)* contrasts with its green-stemmed cousin *Cornus stolonifera* 'Flaviramea', both of which are under-planted with variegated comfrey *(Symphytum grandiflorum)*. The clumps of evergreen ornamental grasses also provide all-year interest *(Carex* 'Silver Sceptre', *Carex elata* 'Aurea' and *Glyceria maxima)*. One of the few flowering plants that does well by the pond in winter is the 'kaffir lily' *(Schizostylis coccinea* and *S. coccinea* 'Alba'*)*. The yellow flowers of the woodland shrub *Mahonia* also provide winter interest.

After the snowdrops and wild garlic, the summer flowers arrive. These include the white plumes of meadowsweet (*Filipendula ulmaria* 'Variegata') and goat's-beard (*Aruncus dioicus*). The yellow spires of *Ligularia* 'The Rocket' and blue irises also thrive in the damp soil. In the dry soil closer to the path, *Euphorbia* 'Redwing', with its interesting foliage, thrives in the shade, as does the beautiful blue poppy, *Meconopsis* x *sheldonii*. Plants like the ornamental rhubarb (*Rheum palmatum*) and *Gunnera manicata*, the much larger plant that looks like a giant rhubarb, but is unrelated, provide bold leaves to contrast with the finer foliage of the other herbaceous plants. Hostas, ferns and angels' fishing rods (*Dierama pulcherrimum*) complete the planting.

*Above: Plants around the pond area include (top) wild garlic or ramsons (*Allium ursinum*). Below: Marsh marigold (*Caltha palustris*)*

The adventure playground

In a sheltered area of Kellie Wood just north of the pond, this is a great place for children of all ages to play, protected from the summer sun and the worst of the westerly winds.

Bird hide

In 2004, a bird hide was created where you can sit and observe the rich diversity of bird life that visits Kellie. Visitors include goldfinch, greenfinch and great spotted woodpecker. It is close to the burn and is surrounded by young hawthorn and rowan trees, with mature elm and yew close by. Nearby, willows will attract birds which come to feed on the insects overwintering in the willow buds.

Crow Wood Cottage

Archibald Constable (see page 6) lived here on the easterly side of the meadow. His house had two storeys and dormer windows, but after a fire broke out in the 1920s it was made into a cottage. The building now provides accommodation for students taking part in the Organic Gardening Studentship at Kellie. The giant copper beech tree in the front garden is the only one on the estate.

Viewpoint

This point in the woodland walk offers a fine view of the castle. John Henry Lorimer was inspired by the picturesque castle and often included it in his paintings. From here you can see a large horse chestnut tree at the edge of Crow Wood – it is close to the fence, about halfway down the boundary of the woods. There is also a magnificent view over the Firth of Forth to the Bass Rock, with its sparkling white coating of guano (droppings) from its famous gannet colony.

*Clockwise from top left:
View of the Bass Rock;
the bird hide; Crow Wood
Cottage*

Caring for wildlife

The woods and landscape around Kellie provide a home for a wide variety of wildlife including foxes, badgers, nesting buzzards and bats. Wherever possible, Trust management encourages these wild residents: for example, repairs around the castle are carried out so that they do not interfere with the pipistrelle bat maternity roost in the building. Nor do we disturb the nests of house martins attached to the windowsills, allowing these summer visitors to enjoy the abundant garden insects. We are also managing the meadow beside the garden for wild flowers and we have not created a path into Crow Wood, on the east side of the estate, so that its rich animal life – including roe deer and buzzards – can live in peace. Elsewhere our management allows visitors regularly to see butterflies and the increasingly rare tree sparrow, feeding around the organic orchard and borders.

The Stables: Hew Lorimer exhibition

The sculptor Hew Lorimer worked in his studio here, open to the elements, until he was in his eighties. The National Trust for Scotland reconstructed the studio in 2002 and it now displays examples of Hew's work.